Making Paper Planes

...that really fly

Making Paper Planes

...that really fly

Nick Robinson

Published by SILVERDALE BOOKS
An imprint of Bookmart Ltd

Registered number 2372865

Trading as Bookmart Ltd
Desford Road
Enderby
Leicester LE19 4AD

© 2003 D&S Books Ltd

D&S Books Ltd
Kerswell,
Parkham Ash, Bideford
Devon, England
EX39 5PR

e-mail us at:-
enquiries@dsbooks.fsnet.co.uk

This edition printed 2003

ISBN 1-856057-32-1

Book Code DS0062 Paper Planes

Creative Director: Sarah King
Editor: Sarah Harris
Project Editor: Judith Millidge
Photographer: Colin Bowling
Designer: Earl Neish

Fonts used: Helvetica, 95 Helvetica Black, Helvetica Black, Times Roman Bold.

Printed in China

1 3 5 7 9 10 8 6 4 2

Contents

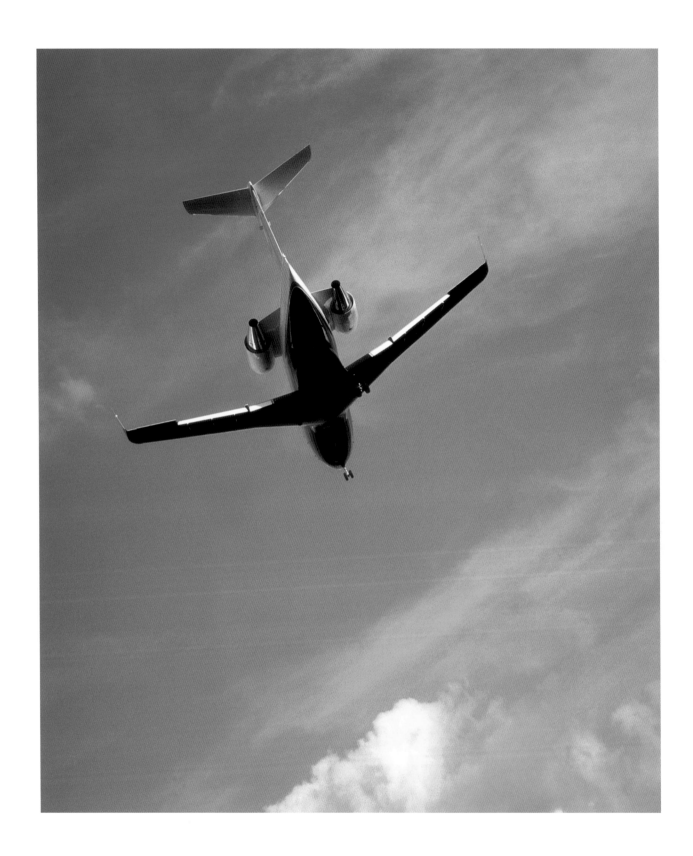

Introduction

The sight of an airplane passing overhead is commonplace these days, yet people still look upwards and watch with fascination as these gleaming machines speed towards their destination. Where does it come from? Where is it going? Who is on board? We know none of these things, yet the simple fact that they are in the air seems to make their trip mysterious and exotic. For most people, airplanes are a fact of life and have always been there, yet the first flight was just 100 years ago. Despite our best efforts, man cannot fly without a machine to help him. However, we can still make other things fly; balloons, gliders, parachutes, and best of all, paper planes.

We don't know when the first paper plane was invented, but the classic 'dart' seems to be over 100 years old. It may have pre-dated the first real plane! As with most paper folding (often known as 'origami'), the economy of means is a major attraction. You only need paper and your hands and within 30 seconds or so, you can create something that can take to the skies. Since they have no engine, paper planes can glide at best. This means they won't stay in the air for long. The current world record for time in the air is less than 30 seconds. One of the designs in this book may well beat that record if you are pre-pared to practise and experiment!

This book aims to take the design of paper planes a small step forward. New techniques for 'locking' the sides of the plane together are used and you are recommended to experiment and extend these ideas. One truth about paper-folding is that just when you think all of the good ideas and designs have already been discovered, somebody finds a new one and you think, 'I wish I'd thought of that!' New ideas are waiting in the paper to be discovered with no more than basic folding skills, some imagination and a bit of dedication.

Making Paper Planes

Making a paper plane that flies well is a mixture of science, experimentation and perseverance. You must be prepared to put some time and effort into it to get the best results. However, it's not beyond anyone to get good results. Here are some of the areas you should think about when reaching for the stars!

People often expect their planes to fly beautifully the first time round. This is very unlikely to happen! In almost all cases, you need to make adjustments to get the best results from your plane, especially if you want to enter any kind of paper plane contest. There are three main areas that may need adjustment. The angle of launch, the speed at which you launch and adjusting (known as 'trimming') the wings. Each of them will have a significant effect upon the quality of flight.

Angle of launch
This refers to the angle that the nose of the plane is pointing at when you let go of it. An angle of zero degrees means launching straight-forward. If you do so, the chances are that the plane will start to sink almost immediately. Most paper planes designed for distance need to be launched with a slight upwards angle. Others might be better with a steep angle of launch so they rise quickly into the air before slowly descending again. This is certainly the case when you are competing for a 'longest time in the air' competition. The idea here is to get as much height as possible, then have the plane fall into a wide circular gliding pattern so that it will take a long time to come down.

Speed of launching
Paper planes with a large wing area usually need a very gentle launch, since the wing area isn't very strong and will buckle if launched too quickly. More streamlined designs can be launched at a faster pace. Some should be launched as quickly as possible! If you want to compete for 'distance' or 'time aloft' records, you'll need to develop an aggressive but controlled launching action. The aim is to impart as much speed as you can without stressing the paper too much. With every plane you fold, experiment to find out the best launch speed. After a while, you will have some idea before you launch, determined by the plane's characteristics.

Trimming
This means adjusting the wings or any other 'sticking out bits'. Probably the most important factor is the angle the wings form from the centre outward. This is known as dihedral. On most designs, you will need a dihedral angle so that the tips of wings are raised relative to the centre of the wings. This will make the plane more stable in flight. The plane may fly better with quite a large angle of dihedral.

How to create an 'A' proportion rectangle

Many of the planes in this book are best made from A4 sized paper. This is easily made from either a square or any other rectangle, as shown below.

'A' proportion from a rectangle

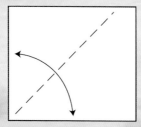

1 Fold one side to an adjacent side, crease and unfold

2 Fold the lower edge to the crease

3 Fold the top edge over, making a crease that touches the corner- crease and unfold

4 Cut along the crease

'A' proportion from a square

1 Fold one side to an adjacent side, crease and unfold

2 Fold the lower edge to the crease

3 Fold the top edge over to meet the end of the crease made in the last step- crease and unfold

4 Cut along the crease

Another key adjustment area is the back of the wings, or 'trailing edges'. If the plane tends to dive too steeply and seems heavy at the nose end, add a very slight upwards curl to the back of the wings. Be sure to make any adjustments small ones, giving the plane a test launch after each one. You will soon learn the right amount of 'tweak' to apply to the wing.

To confuse matters, these three factors will affect each others. Launching more slowly, you may need a greater dihedral. Curling the wing-tips you may need a steeper angle of launch. The only way to find out is to make a single change, then fly the plane and watch how it performs. Keep adjusting until you have fine-tuned the plane. After a while, you will learn to do this quickly and will know how to cure various flight problems.

Conditions
Paper planes are usually very lightweight and so are easily affected by wind. The only sensible answer to this problem is to fly your planes indoors and keep all windows and doors shut. Good locations include gymnasiums, halls, large garages, and so on. An ideal location has no wind or draughts, a length of 300 feet and a height of 100 feet. The only place you can find this is in sports arenas or aircraft hangars, which can prove expensive to hire, but it is worth it. You can then break some world records!

Paper has a tendency to absorb moisture from the air. This means your plane's wings will start to sag after a while. There is no cure for this (other than a warm, dry room) so you should be prepared to 'retire' your plane after a fairly limited lifespan. You should then fold another! The frustrating part is that no matter how carefully you fold two apparently identical planes, one may be a great flier, the other hopeless. This is part of the fun, since if it were easy to predict flight characteristics, the whole process would become mechanical. The reality of the situation is that a raw beginner can strike lucky and get very impressive results.

Optional extras
Many paper plane enthusiasts are quite strict when making paper planes; they will only use folding techniques to achieve their results. Others will use sticky tape, weights, cuts, extra pieces, anything it takes to help the plane fly. The rules for the paper plane world record (both for distance and for time in the air), allow you to use small pieces of tape to keep the wings together.

A few years ago, following a suggestion from the British Origami Society, a new category was added, which insists on the use of pure origami techniques with no cuts or use of tape. This has encouraged many paper-folders to have a go at designing paper planes: some of the exciting designs are featured within this book. Many children like to tear small flaps in the wings to make it look better and possibly improve the flight. The use of flaps can certainly allow you to make fine adjustments to the 'trim' of the plane, but you may feel that it is less satisfactory than 'pure' folding.

Tips for folding from this book

Make sure your hands are clean before folding!

Fold on a flat surface, such as a table.

Don't rush the model - fold slowly, carefully and neatly.

If you don't quite understand the photos, read the words as well.

Make each plane three times - the last should fly much more effectively than the first!

Be creative – alter angles and distances to see if you can improve the flight pattern.

Everyone has his or her own standards and you should do whatever makes you happy! It is also true that adding some weight to the front end of a plane (in the form of a paper clip) will often make it fly better, but you may think that is a bit of a cheat.

Choosing paper

The choice of paper patterns is entirely up to you, but be warned that some types of paper (for example, sugar paper) do not make very good planes, since it isn't crisp enough. Some types of paper will absorb moisture from the air more quickly and should be avoided. If the design is very complicated, you may need thinner paper, as above a certain size, the plane simply won't fly at all.

Standard European A4 paper or American photocopy letter size is perfect for most uses and is cheap to buy. Tracing paper is light, but strong, making it great for planes. Here is how you create A4 proportioned paper from a different shaped rectangle or a square (see p.10).

Creating your own designs

When you fold the more complicated paper planes, you might be in awe of the people who created them. They might seem talented and artistic, but this isn't always the case. Many simply adapt ideas from other designs and add a few new touches. If you start with a simple design, you can alter distances, change some of the angles, add extra creases and miss some creases. Eventually, you'll have an original design!

When testing your designs, carry out test flights after each change to see what effect it had. If it flies properly, you have adapted it successfully. If not, start with a new sheet and try some different changes. Don't keep altering the same model, since the paper will have many unwanted creases. Since paper is so cheap, it will cost very little! If you know someone who works in an office, they probably throw away hundreds of sheets of paper every week. A polite request should get you as much folding material as you need.

There is no simple route to being creative, but you must have patience and be prepared to break any rules that get in your way. For example, most planes start by folding the long edges of the paper together. Why not try the opposite - fold the short edges together instead? Designs such as the 'Landscape' and the 'Alison' start this way. You may find problems that will need ingenuity and patience to solve, but your designs are more likely to be original. Something else you might like to try is the 'Holy Grail' of paper planes: asymmetrical designs. These are shapes that are not symmetrical – the wings may be a different shape. Many say it is impossible to create such a plane, but who knows?

Competitions

If you are serious about paper planes, you'll want to challenge some of the world records by entering or setting up competitions. There are a number of categories for which there are international records. These include 'time aloft', (how long can you keep your plane in the air (this is currently over 20 seconds) and 'distance', how far you can make a paper plane travel. (The current record stands at nearly 60 meters). Many professional competitors use small lengths of sticky tape to keep the sides of the plane together. However, there is now an official category for 'origami', where the design must only use folding techniques. World record holders take their hobby very seriously and put in hours of practice, building up the specific muscles that are used to launch a plane. If you want to hold a competition at work or school, all you really need is a large open space with no wind. To attempt a world record, you'll need a large aircraft hangar! You can also organise less serious categories such as acrobatics, most decorative design, worst flyer(!) and most entertaining launch technique.

Societies

Around the world, you'll find small groups of people who are devoted to paper planes. You may have more success by joining origami societies. There is at least one in every major country in the world. You will be able read a regular magazine, buy proper paper and get your hands on books featuring paper planes. Perhaps most importantly, you'll make contact with lots of other people who enjoy paper-folding. People who do origami (the Japanese word for paper-folding) are usually very friendly and will help you with any folding problems you may have. Many origamists are keen paper-plane flyers in their spare time. Here are two of the largest web-sites.

British Origami Society www.britishorigami.org.uk

Origami USA www.ousa.com

At the time of writing, the current records are:

TIME ALOFT

Guinness World Record	**27.6** seconds set by *Ken Blackburn* 1998	
Guinness British Record	**20.9** seconds set by *Chris Edge & Andy Currey* 28th July 1996	
Origami Record	**20.9** seconds set by *Andy Currey* 28th July 1996	

DISTANCE

Guinness World Record	**193** feet (58.8m) set by *Tony Fletch* 21st May 1985	
Guinness British Record	**104** feet (31.7m) set by *Andy Currey* 19th September 1997	
Origami Record	**94** feet (28.7m) set by *Robin Glynne* 19th September 1997	

Glossary of Aviation Terms

Aileron: a moveable part of an aeroplane's wing, which makes an aeroplane roll.

Airfoil: the wing of an aeroplane, which produces lift.

Angle of attack: The angle at which the wings meet the air.

Asymmetrical: a design with wings that are a different shape to each other.

Barnstormer: a plane designed to perform aerobatics.

Canard: a design where the tail is at the front rather than the rear.

Centre of gravity: the point at which a plane balances.

Control surfaces: moveable parts of the plane that control flight.

Elevator: a part of the tail which tilts an aeroplane up or down.

Flight pattern: the path a plane makes through the air.

Fuselage: the main body of the plane.

Laminar-flow wing: a wing that creates less air resistance (drag) than a normal wing.

Leading edges: the front edges of a wing.

Lift: a force which acts on the wings to move the plane upward.

Mach number: mach 1 is the speed of sound.

Pitch: when the tail of the plane moves the up or down.

Trailing edges: the back edges of the wing.

Ornithopter: old-fashioned type of flying machine that looks like a bird.

Rudder: the vertical part of a tail.

Roll: when one wing moves up as the other moves down.

Rate of roll: the speed the aeroplane rolls.

Stable: when a plane flies straight and level without rolling, pitching or yawing.

Stall: when the plane loses control and drops from the sky!

Supersonic: an airplane capable of exceeding the speed of sound.

Swept-wing: a design where leading and trailing edges of a wing point backward.

Unstable: when a plane changes direction without control.

VTOL Vertical Take Off & Landing - an aircraft that can fly straight upwards.

Yaw: when one wing moves forward as the other moves backwards.

Wing tip: the outer end of an airplane's wing.

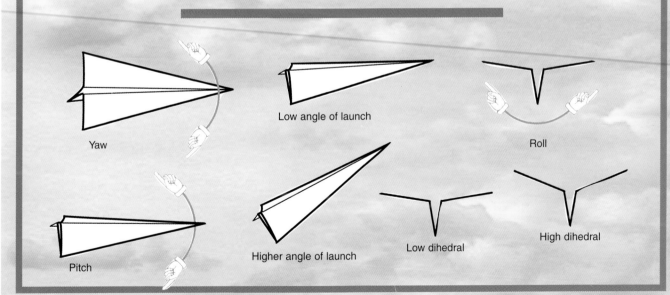

Yaw

Low angle of launch

Roll

Pitch

Higher angle of launch

Low dihedral

High dihedral

The Projects

The projects in this book should ideally be folded in order, since some of the later designs may present less detailed explanation of moves and techniques that are covered in earlier designs. More experienced folders may pick and choose. Remember to fold slowly and carefully, checking ahead to see what you are aiming for with each step. Make your first few models using any paper you can lay your hands on. Once you've mastered the sequence, you might want to use slightly better quality paper.

Turnover symbol

Classic Dart

There can be few people who have never enjoyed the pleasure
of launching this simple design. No-one knows exactly
how old it is, but it may even pre-date the first 'real' aeroplane!
It's a good opportunity to practise making neat, accurate creases. As
with all paper models, if you take your time, the result
will look much more impressive.

2 Fold the lower left-hand
corner in so that the short edge
lies along the central crease.
The completed fold is shown on
the other side.

1 Fold one long side to meet
the other, adjust until they are
perfectly lined up. Hold the layers
in position with one hand, then
crease firmly and unfold.

3 Make a similar fold by taking
the folded edge to meet the
central crease. The completed
fold is shown on the other side.
Remember to make sharp
creases.

4 Fold the plane in half along the central crease to produce this step.

5 Fold the wing tip to meet the original half-way crease. Turn the paper round so that you can fold away from yourself, as this makes life easier.

6 This is the result. Repeat the fold with the other wing.

7 Because this design has a sharp point at one end, it might be dangerous to fly towards people. To make it safer, it's a good idea to cut or tear the sharp point off. You'll be surprised to see that this produces a mini-plane!

FLIGHT ADVICE

Launch
Medium-strength at a slight upwards angle.

Trim
The wings should have .a slight upward angle (dihedral).

Creative suggestions
Try turning the paper over before step 3. Try folding in half using a mountain crease in step 4.

8 Complete!

Classic Glider

This is another tried-and-tested design. The idea of 'locking'
the flaps together using the triangular tab was first suggested
by a Japanese paper plane expert called Eiji Nakamura.
When trimmed properly, it is a superb glider, yet it is
simple and quick to make.

1 Fold one long side to meet
the other, crease firmly and
unfold.

2 Fold both halves of a short
edge to lie along the central
crease, as with the Classic Dart.
Leave a small 'fudge factor' (see
next step).

3 Because paper planes can
often be several layers thick, folding in half towards the final
stages can be awkward. To help,
we often leave a small gap when
folding in to the central crease.
American folders refer to this as
a 'fudge factor'.

4 Fold the end of the triangle to the right, almost to the end of the central crease, leaving a gap about as wide as your thumb (it isn't critical). Refer to the next picture for guidance.

5 Fold a corner to lie along the central crease, but move it slightly to the left before creasing. This creates a small gap on the left-hand side, making it safer to throw in a crowd! The completed fold is shown on the other side.

6 Swing the small triangle to the left, overlapping the two corners. This 'locks' them in place during flight.

7 Mountain-fold the plane in half, swinging the lower half underneath.

8 This is the result. Turn the paper around.

9 Starting at the corner of the blunted nose, fold the wings past the lower edge. Refer to the next picture for guidance.

10 This is the result – the hidden edge is shown in x-ray view. Repeat with the other wing.

11 Complete.

FLIGHT ADVICE

Launch
Medium-strength at a slight upwards angle.

Trim
The wings should have slight upward angle (dihedral).

Creative suggestions
Alter the fold used to create the wings in step 10, making the wings firstly bigger, then smaller. How does this affect the flight? If you don't 'lock' the flaps, does it make a difference?

Hawk

This is another design with a long history, having been around since at least the 1930s. It uses an elegant series of origami techniques to create the nose section. You should make this design several times until you are confident about the folding method. Start with the central crease in place.

2 Repeat the fold to the other long edge - the picture shows this step before unfolding.

1 Fold a short edge over to meet a long edge. Crease firmly and unfold.

3 Open the paper out. Turn the paper over so that the creases you have made are now mountain folds.

MAKING PAPER PLANES

6 This is the result. The triangular section is known as a 'waterbomb base' in the origami world.

4 Fold the corners to meet the ends of the diagonal creases. Crease and unfold.

5 Turn the paper over and use the creases to collapse the paper into a triangular shape.

7 Fold one of the loose corners to the tip of the triangle.

8 Repeat on the other corner. This is the result.

9 Turn the paper around to this position. Fold the two loose corners to the opposite corner of the internal square, taking the layer underneath with them. Crease carefully (due to the thickness) and unfold.

11 Repeat the last step with the lower-right side of the square. Repeat the last two steps on the upper side of the square.

10 Turn the paper back to the previous position. Fold one side of the square to meet the horizontal crease. Crease and unfold.

12 Fold in two upper sides of the square, pressing the centre together into a point. Repeat on the other side.

14 This is the result. Valley-fold in half along the central crease.

13 Turn the paper over and fold the tip in on an existing crease. The crease is a mountain, which you'll need to change to a valley. Fold carefully and enjoy the way the folds move into position.

15 This is the result.

MAKING PAPER PLANES

16 Fold one of the wings down, parallel to the lower edge, starting at the top of the nose section.

17 Then fold it back up level with the base of the plane.

18 Fold back down once more and repeat with the other wing. You can experiment with the position of these pleats.

FLIGHT ADVICE

Launch
Hold underneath by the bulky section. Launch firmly, either straight forward or directly upwards.

Trim
The creases on the wings should be symmetrical.

Creative suggestions
Try lots of different ways to crease the wings; add more creases, also try fewer creases.

19 Complete.

Test Plane

by **Nick Robinson.**
This design will help you explore the effect that
various wing configurations can have upon the flight pattern.
You can use these ideas when exploring variations of
the other designs in the book.

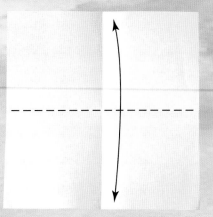

2 Fold two corners to the centre, crease and unfold.

1 Start with a square creased in half. Fold in half, crease and unfold.

3 Fold two edges in to meet the creases made in the last step. Swing both flaps over on existing creases.

MAKING PAPER PLANES

5 Rotate the paper. Follow the creases shown to form a central point, which you swing downwards.

4 Fold one side over along the inside edge. Repeat with the other flap, leaving it in place.

6 Pull out the layer of paper from within the layers.

8 Fold the whole coloured section over on an existing crease.

7 Tuck the layer underneath.

9 Fold the paper in half.

10 Fold both wings down to form a narrow body.

11 This is the basic shape to which you can add variations.

12 Here, two wingtips have been folded up. Try folding them down and compare.

13 Further creases make a more complicated profile.

14 You can go as far as you like, but try each step to see if it helps the flight, or hinders it.

FLIGHT ADVICE

Launch
Experiment!

Trim
Experiment!

Creative suggestions
Experiment!

How to hold your plane

Canard

Traditional, arranged by **Nick Robinson.**
This is a well known variation on the traditional dart, where the original corners are allowed to point out instead of being folded away. The term *canard* (which is French for 'duck') refers to aircraft with some kind of stabilisers at the front end.

1 Start with an A4 or similar rectangle, creased in half. Fold two corners to the centre.

2 Turn the paper over and take the folded edges to the centre, allowing the corners to pop out again. Unfold these flaps.

3 Fold the lower left-hand edge to the crease you made in the last step. This step is not used in the traditional design.

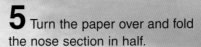

5 Turn the paper over and fold the nose section in half.

4 Refold the flaps on existing creases.

6 This is the result; fold in half.

7 Fold both wings down to the long folded edge.

8 Complete.

FLIGHT ADVICE

Launch
Launch gently at a slight upward angle.

Trim
The flaps at the front and the wings will interact with each other.

Creative suggestions
Can you make another plane with a canard design?

How to hold your plane

Championship

Traditional.
This is the basic design used by many of the current record-breakers in the paper airplane world, to which they add a strip of tape to keep the wings together. As you will see, it flies beautifully without the tape.

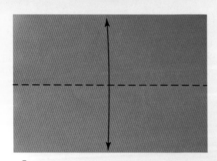

1 Start with an A4 rectangle. Fold one long side to meet the other, crease firmly and unfold.

2 Fold the left-hand corners to lie along the central crease. Don't forget a small fudge factor.

3 Fold the triangular shape over along the inside edge.

4 Fold two corners in as in step two, then unfold both sides.

5 Mountain-fold the plane in half. Fold the corner over at a slight angle, starting at the end of the crease. Turn over and match the other side up.

6 Open back to the start of step four. With the small creases in place, refold the existing creases.

7 This is the result. Fold the small triangular flap over to 'lock' the loose flaps, then mountain-fold the plane in half.

8 Mountain-fold the plane in half again. Fold the wings down: the crease starts at the tip of the nose and passes through the top of the tiny triangle.

9 Complete.

FLIGHT ADVICE

Launch
Launch with a firm forward release, try all different angles of release.

Trim
As ever, adjust the wing angles.

Creative suggestions
Alter the angle at which the wings are folded down in step 8.

How to hold your plane

Hoop

By *Nick Robinson*

There are very few circular designs that fly. This one is a variation on a similar traditional design made from a square of paper.

1 Start with a sheet of A4 or similar rectangle. Fold the bottom left corner to meet the top right corner.

2 Fold in half along the folded edge.

3 Like this. Crease firmly and unfold completely.

4 You have now created a crease which runs from corner to opposite corner. Fold along that crease.

5 Make a pinch mark to locate the half-way point of the central crease.

6 Take the folded edge to meet the pinch mark.

7 Carefully fold the outside edge to the inside edge. Crease and unfold.

8 Form the paper into a tube and start to feed one end into the other.

9 Finally, refold the crease made in step seven to lock the paper together. Make sure to hold the interlocking flaps together as you start this.

10 Once in place, run your fingers around the edge to make it smooth and circular.

11 Complete.

FLIGHT ADVICE

Launch
The thin part of the loop should be on top – hold by the sides or the lower rear end and push it forwards at medium speed.

Creative suggestions
Alter the amount folded in during steps 6 and 7. Try to make the same design starting with a square.

How to hold your plane

Radford

By **Nick Robinson**

This attractive sequence of folds creates a glider that performs
very well. It was named in memory of Mark Radford,
an origami friend of the author.

1 Start with a sheet of A4,
creased in half. Fold a corner in
to lie along the central crease.
Repeat with the matching corner.

2 Fold the tip in to meet the
two corners.

3 Swing the thicker section
back over along the inside raw
edges.

5 Fold the outer edges of the wings to lie along the central crease. Crease and unfold.

4 Turn the paper over. If you flatten the paper, you'll be able to see the hidden edge underneath. Fold the tips of the thicker section to touch the central crease at this point.

6 Reverse the direction of the creases to fold the small sections underneath.

8 Complete.

7 Form the classic paper plane profile using existing creases.

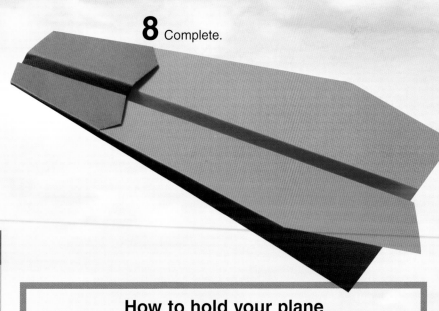

FLIGHT ADVICE

Launch
Medium-strength at a slight upwards angle.

Trim
The wings should have a slight upward angle (dihedral).

Creative suggestions
Alter the distances in steps 2 and 3.

How to hold your plane

Flying Square

By **Nick Robinson**

This design is unusual, in that it starts with a square and finishes with a square! The design arranges internal layers of paper towards the front, so that the centre of gravity will allow for a gliding flight.

2 Turn the paper round 90 degrees and fold in half from corner to corner again. The picture shows the finished step.

1 Start with a square, white side upwards. Fold in half from corner to corner, crease and unfold.

3 Fold the left-hand corner to the top corner. The completed fold is shown on the right.

4 Fold the right-hand triangle in half towards you. The completed fold is shown on the left.

5 Fold the upper edge of the right-hand triangular section to meet the outside edge. The completed fold is shown on the other side.

6 Open the paper out completely and turn to the white side. Alter the creases shown to match the direction indicated.

7 Start to form the paper into a 3D shape, bringing the furthest corner towards you. The paper will collapse into a small square. Refer to the next picture for guidance.

8 This should be the result. If not, unfold and check you have used the correct mountain and valley creases. Use existing creases to fold the small flaps into a pocket.

9 One flap is in place, the other is being tucked in.

10 Curl the edges upwards to complete.

FLIGHT ADVICE

Launch
Hold by the rear corner, above your head and launch with a gentle forward release. Try it from a high building!

Trim
The outer wingtips should be curled upwards.

How to hold your plane

Sallas

By **Nick Robinson**

This design is named after a talented German creator called Joan Sallas. It starts with a smaller sheet of paper than the usual A4. You can also try many of the other designs in the book from smaller paper, to see how they perform.

1 Start with a sheet of A5 (half A4) or similar rectangle, creased in half. Fold the short edges together, pinching the centre point.

2 Fold a corner to lie exactly on the centre point.

3 Repeat with the other corner.

5 Turn the paper over, then fold each half of the short edge to the central crease.

4 Now fold the tip to the same place.

6 Fold the plane in half.

7 Fold the wing over along the crease shown.

8 Complete.

FLIGHT ADVICE

Launch
Moderate speed, straight forward.

Trim
Keep the wings almost horizontal.

Creative suggestions
Alter the angles of the wings.

How to hold your plane

Triplane

By **Nick Robinson**

Unlike most paper planes, this design uses a 60 degree geometry. It is quite easy to create this angle and there will be many exciting designs waiting to be discovered using these techniques.

1 Start with a square, folded in half. Fold in both sides to the central crease.

2 This is the result. Turn the paper over.

3 Fold one edge to the central crease and make a gentle crease about one third the length of the paper.

4 Make a crease that starts in the middle of the short edge. The corner you fold in should just touch the crease you made in the last step.

6 Open the paper out fully: you can see the 60 degree triangles formed. Fold in making your crease pass through the inside corners of the triangles.

5 Rotate the paper and fold the other corner to lie along the crease made in the last step.

7 Using existing creases, fold one corner in, flattening the out-side point.

9 Pull out a layer of paper to tuck the point within a pocket underneath.

8 Repeat the move with the other corner.

43

MAKING PAPER PLANES

11 Take the folded front edge of the wing to lie along the centre. Repeat with the other wing.

10 Fold the point over.

12 Form the classic plane profile to complete the design.

14 Complete.

How to hold your plane

The Alison

By **Nick Robinson**

This is a slow, stable glider, which doesn't use the familiar 'short sides to the centre' technique of many planes. Instead, the paper is folded in half, then half of the paper is tucked back into the nose section to generate the proper centre of gravity.

2 Fold the raw edges to the central crease.

1 Start with a sheet of A4 or similar rectangle, creased in half between the long edges. Fold the two short edges together.

3 Fold the short edges of the left-hand layers back to the long edges, crease and unfold.

MAKING PAPER PLANES

4 Swing open the first of the layers, pressing the top corner into a triangle, using existing creases.

5 Swing the central section to the left.

6 Fold the lower edge to touch the upper edge of the section you have just folded. Repeat other side.

7 Turn the paper over and fold the smaller flap over the folded edge, crease and unfold to step five.

8 Using the creases you added in steps five and seven, tuck the central flap into the pocket.

9 Refold the central crease through the nose section and adjust the profile to that shown in the final image.

FLIGHT ADVICE

Launch
Hold the plane gently by the centre. Launch with a gentle forward push.

Trim
Adjust the various angles of the wings.

Creative suggestions
Can you find an imaginative way of using the 'spare' paper in step eight?

How to hold your plane

Stump

By **Nick Robinson**

This is another example of how a traditional design can be worked upon to incorporate new ideas. Here, some of the surplus paper at the nose end is overlapped to lock the nose section together and make the design more stable in flight.

1 Start with an A4 or similar rectangle, creased in half. Fold one short edge over to both sides, as in the Hawk.

2 Turn the paper over and fold the short edge to the end of the creases.

3 Turn back over again and use the creases to collapse the paper into the familiar triangular form.

MAKING PAPER PLANES

4 Fold the tips of the triangles into the centre.

5 Fold the outer corners in to the centre.

6 Fold the outer corner of the square section in to the centre and make a horizontal crease the full length of the plane. There are many layers, so fold carefully. Repeat on the other side.

7 Fold the nose into the centre of the square section.

8 Fold the lower-left edge of the central square to the centre. Repeat on the other side, but leave a large fudge factor to allow for the thickness of the paper.

9 Fold the body in half and tuck one flap over the other to lock the body together.

10 Fold the wings down.

11 Then fold the wingtips back up.

12 Complete!

FLIGHT ADVICE

Launch
Gentle to moderate speed, directly forward.

Trim
Adjust the wing angles.

Creative suggestions
Try radical changes to the wing profile.

How to hold your plane

49

Star Fighter

By **Nick Robinson**

This design makes use of the two layers of paper created in the first step to create double-sided wingtips. There are very few designs which create this type of wing profile – why not try to create one of your own?

1 Start with an A4 or similar rectangle, creased in half. Fold the two short edges together.

2 Take each half of the folded edge to the centre, crease firmly and unfold.

3 Fold the edge to the crease made in the last step, then unfold again.

4 Alter the creases as necessary, making the longest one a mountain and the shorter one a valley, on both layers of paper. If you then re-form the creases, the paper will collapse into the position shown. Look at the picture closely!

6 Fold the whole model in half.

7 Make a crease to form the body. The exact position isn't critical. You can also do this in two stages by folding each wing separately.

5 Repeat on the other wing.

9 Swing the flap over once more.

8 Fold the tip of the nose to the point where the hidden layers meet inside.

10 Use the edges of the nose section as a reference to fold the sides of the wings to. You should repeat this on the three other flaps.

11 Open out into the profile shown. Complete.

FLIGHT ADVICE

Launch
Launch at speed, at most angles.

Trim
Keep the wings at right angles to the body, adjust the wing tips symmetrically.

Creative suggestions
Try alternative wing profiles.

How to hold your plane

Landscape

By *Nick Robinson*

This plane is so called because unlike most paper airplanes,
it uses a sheet of paper which is in the 'landscape' format
(wider than high). Most designs start with the paper in 'portrait' format. If
you are wanting to create truly original designs,
this layout is more likely to get you results!

1 Start with a sheet of A4 or similar rectangle, creased in half between the short edges. Take the bottom right corner to the top centre, crease firmly and unfold.

2 Fold the outside edge to the crease you have just made, crease and unfold.

3 Repeat step one on the left-hand side.

4 Make a valley fold from the bottom left corner to the end of the crease on the upper surface.

6 Using the existing creases, swing the paper over and tuck it underneath the layers on the right.

5 Make a fold similar to step two on the left-hand side.

7 Mountain-fold the paper in half.

9 Fold the wing back at a slight angle so that the corner of the wing-tip is behind the rear edge of the plane.

8 Fold most of the wing away from you – the exact distance isn't critical.

10 Fold the tip back again, so that the rear edge of this tip is vertical.

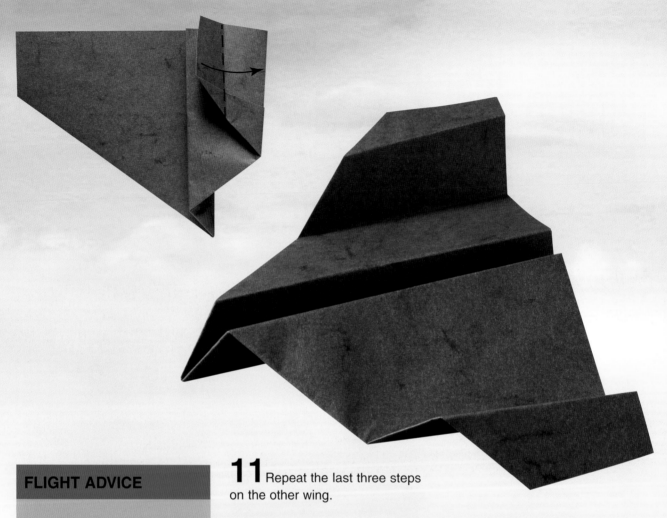

FLIGHT ADVICE

11 Repeat the last three steps on the other wing.

Launch
Open the wings to match the final photograph. Launch with medium strength at a slight upwards angle.

Trim
The end section of the wings should be at the same angle as the largest wing section.

Creative suggestions
Starting at step 8, create your own design!

How to hold your plane

Lock Glider

By **Nick Robinson**

The body (or fuselage) of most paper airplanes tends to open during flight. However, using some origami ingenuity, it is possible to lock the nose together to prevent this.

1 Start with an A4 or similar rectangle. Fold the two long sides together, crease and unfold.

2 Fold the two left-hand corners in to the centre crease. Leave a slight fudge factor.

3 Now fold the wings in once more, as in the traditional Dart. Unfold again.

4 Fold part of the raw edge to lie along the crease made in the last step.

5 Refold step three.

6 Fold the edges of the nose section to lie along the centre crease, but only crease from the tail section as far as the folded edges.

7 Mountain- fold the nose behind – the fold passes through the point where the creases made in the last step meet the folded edges.

8 Turn the paper over. Fold the sharp tip back to the inside of the triangular section.

9 Valley-fold the whole plane in half.

10 Fold the tip of the nose over along an inside edge – you should be able to both see and feel this edge. Crease and unfold.

11 Open the top of the plane and push the triangular flap inside using the crease you made in the last step. Lift the left-hand flap up and tuck the paper underneath.

MAKING PAPER PLANES

13 ...the step complete. You should be able to refold the plane in half again, with the nose section locked.

12 In progress...

14 Complete.

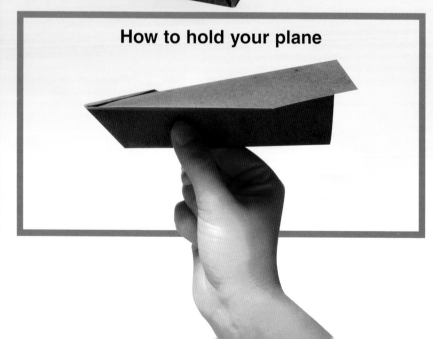

FLIGHT ADVICE

Launch
Medium-strength, at a slight upwards angle.

Trim
Alter the angle of the wings to the body. Make sure the rear corners of the wings are not curled up or down.

Creative suggestions
In step 6, make a fold at right angles to the tail to create a thin, equal body shape. Continue as before. This variation should be a slow glider.

How to hold your plane

Needle Dart

By **Nick Robinson**

This is an ultra-modern design, sleek and stylish. It uses the 'squash' technique taken from traditional origami.

1 Start with an A4 rectangle or similar, creased in half.Fold two corners to the centre.

2 Take the folded edges to the centre as well.

3 Turn the paper over and fold the edges of the sharp end to the centre. These creases only need to extend about one third of the length.

MAKING PAPER PLANES

4 Fold the tip to the centre of the opposite end.

5 Fold the same point back along the hidden inside edges formed in step one.

6 Fold the edges of the pointed flap in to the centre, carefully squashing the paper at the end. See the next picture for guidance. Repeat with the other side.

7 Fold the short edge underneath the point in half.

8 Fold in half along the centre.

9 Fold the wings back down on the line formed by the top of the pointed nose. Crease and unfold.

11 Push the tail inside the body, so it sticks out the other side.

10 Pre-crease a tail flap.

12 Complete.

FLIGHT ADVICE

Launch
A steady speed, slightly upwards.

Trim
As ever, the wings.

Creative suggestions
Try alternative wing profiles.

How to hold your plane

The Swift

By *Kunihiko Kasahara*

Kasahara is one of the foremost origami designers in the world. Here, he turns his skills to creating a highly acrobatic stunt plane, which swoops and turns just like a swift in flight.

2 Fold one end of the crease to meet the pinch mark.

1 Start with a square, creased in half. Fold one end of the crease to the other, pinching lightly to find the centre point.

3 Fold both corners over to meet the inside raw edge.

4 Fold each half of the nearest (folded) edge to lie along the vertical centre crease. Leave a slight fudge factor.

5 Make a horizontal valley fold which passes through the original pinch mark.

6 Fold the tip back outwards. The exact distance isn't critical.

7 Carefully mountain-fold in half on the original central crease.

8 Make a crease which starts at the half-way point of the raw edge on the right and passes through the internal angle formed by the coloured sections. Make sure you have this clear in your mind before folding! Repeat with the other wing.

9 Pre-crease a valley fold which will form the tail fin.

63

MAKING PAPER PLANES

10 Push in the tail section using the creases shown. Reinforce the wing creases.

11 Make a valley crease between the two corners shown to shape the wings.

12 Complete.

FLIGHT ADVICE

Launch
AS fast as possible, straight upwards!

Trim
Alter the relative angle of the wings to the wingtips.

Creative suggestions
Try folding the wingtips down instead of up.

How to hold your plane

The Martin

By **Rikki Donachie**

This is a very clever design, with a neat, flowing sequence. It ends up with two small flaps with which you can launch it.

2 Take each folded edge to the inside raw edge, creasing as far as the centre.

1 Start with a sheet of A4 creased in half. Fold two corners to the central crease at one end.

3 Take each folded edge to the centre, creasing as far as the previous fold.

4 Turn the paper over and fold the triangular section over.

MAKING PAPER PLANES

5 Use existing creases to flatten the paper into a point. Two small mountain creases are formed as you flatten the paper.

6 This is the result. Turn the paper over.

7 Fold the two outside corners to the centre.

8 Fold the model in half from side to side.

9 Fold the wings over, bisecting the angle of the nose.

10 Fold out two small flaps, with which you can launch the plane.

11 Complete.

FLIGHT ADVICE

Launch
Open the body slightly and hold by the two fins. Adjust the wings to be at right angles to the body. Launch with medium strength.

Trim
Check the wings are perfectly flat.

Creative suggestions
Can you create a new plane starting at step seven?

How to hold your plane

Spinner

By **Nick Robinson**

This design is more like a sycamore seed than a paper plane,
but just as much fun to fly!

2 Turn the paper over and fold
in half from side to opposite side.
Repeat once more to form the
'Union Jack' crease pattern.

1 Start with a square,
coloured side up. Fold in
half from one corner to the
opposite corner, repeat with
the other two corners.

3 Fold one corner in to the
centre of the paper – the
completed fold is shown on
the other side.

4 Collapse the paper using
existing creases only.

MAKING PAPER PLANES

5 This is the result. Fold an outside corner into the centre of the paper. Repeat on the matching corner and the two corners underneath.

6 Narrow the flaps by folding to the centre, once again repeating the fold on the three matching flaps.

7 This is the result - fold one layer upwards, turn the paper over and repeat on the matching flap.

8 You should now have flat sections of paper top and bottom. Fold one of the loose flaps over at 45 degrees.

9 This is the result. Repeat underneath.

10 Complete!

FLIGHT ADVICE

Launch
Hold the model as high as possible and release.

Trim
Adjust the angles of the 'wing' flaps.

Creative suggestions
Try making the flaps wider or more narrow.

How to hold your spinner

Art Deco Wing

By **_Michael LaFosse_**

This is a flying wing design, something that is quite hard to achieve using paper. LaFosse is a highly gifted creator and has produced many stunning origami pieces, as well as many unusual and interesting flying designs.

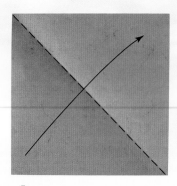

1 Start with a square of paper. Fold from corner to corner.

2 Fold both ends of the folded edge to the top corner.

3 Take the left-hand vertical edge to the outside edge, crease and unfold.

4 Lift and squash using the crease you have just made.

69

5 Repeat on the other side.

6 Turn the paper over and fold the large triangular flap over.

7 Fold the smaller triangular flap upwards, tucking it into the pocket.

8 Rotate the paper to the position shown. Fold the triangular flap in half.

9 Fold the same section in half again.

10 Swing the flap over again.

11 Rotate the paper. Fold the two small outside corners to lie along the horizontal edge.

12 Rotate the paper once more. Tuck the flap inside the pocket.

13 Again, rotate the paper. Getting dizzy? Lift the central flap and fold it upwards. At the same time, fold the paper on either side inwards, allowing it to flatten neatly. Check the next picture for help.

14 This is the result - tuck the paper into the pocket underneath.

FLIGHT ADVICE

Launch
Hold the plane in the centre, from behind. Launch with a gentle forward push.

Trim
Adjust the two fins.

Creative suggestions
Create your own flying wing using step six as a starting point.

15 Finally, add two small mountain folds to form fins.

How to hold your plane

Rocket

by **Nick Robinson**

Identical in shape to an existing non-flying design, this fold
actually flies. You can also have fun placing a box in the garden,
then trying to drop the rocket into it from
as far away as possible.

1 Start with a large square
of paper. Crease both
diagonals.

2 Turn the paper over and
fold in half from side to
side, both ways.

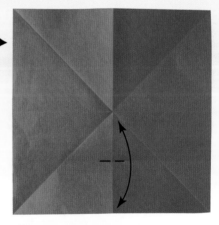

3 Turn back over and add a
small crease marking the
half-way point.

5 Repeat on all four corners to produce this crease pattern. Turn the paper over.

4 Fold the central crease to touch the mark made in the last step. Crease right across the paper.

6 Fold a corner over, so that the location points shown meet up. Check the next picture for guidance.

7 Like this. Make a small crease between the points shown. Then turn the paper back over.

8 All these creases are in the paper, but you will need to alter some as shown. Twist the centre of the paper anti-clockwise as it collapses into the position shown in the next diagram.

9 Here is the move in progress. Make sure you are only folding the creases shown and not adding any new ones!

10 Well done. Fold the loose layer at the top-left downwards.

11 Swing the hidden layer up from beneath, so that the paper is symmetrical.

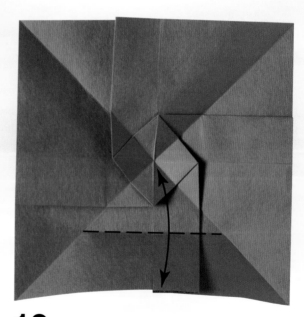

12 Crease the half-way point of the lower triangular section. Repeat on the three other sides.

13 Imagine the paper is a plain square and collapse it into the water bomb base.

14 Take one of the folded edges to the vertical centre edge, crease firmly and unfold.

15 Swing the corner up and right, starting at the centre of the lower edge. The crease passes through a meeting point of two creases (shown in grey). See the next picture for guidance.

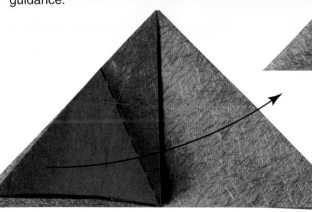

16 Collapse the paper using the creases indicated. Once again, use the next picture as a guide.

75

MAKING PAPER PLANES

17 This is the result, all being well! Swing the small flap to the left, crease & unfold.

18 Repeat the last four steps on the three remaining flaps, then arrange the layers into a cross, with each flap at 45 degrees to the next. Complete!

How to hold your plane

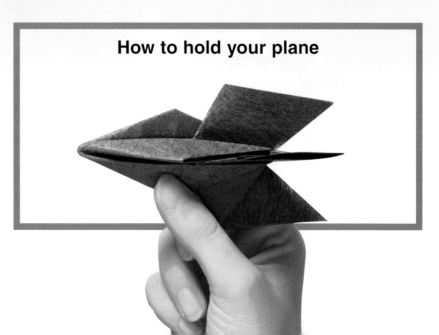

FLIGHT ADVICE

Launch

This design should be thrown as hard as possible at about 45 degrees. A higher angle will produce a shorter distance.

The Twin

By *Nick Robinson*

This shows how, with a bit of imagination, exciting new designs can be developed from existing ones. This one uses the Landscape (page 52) and Canard (page 30) designs and with minor adaptations, joins them into a flying model you couldn't achieve using a single sheet.

Start with the Landscape design folded up to step seven, then unfolded completely and the Canard folded to completion, then unfolded to step five.

1 Make a horizontal crease which joins the main crease intersections on either side.

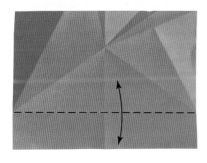

2 Fold the lower corners over so that their inside edges meet the two existing creases.

3 Swing the lower section over on the crease made in step one.

4 Take the Canard and fold the tip of the upper square in half towards you. Then mountain-fold the rest of it behind on an existing (valley) crease.

MAKING PAPER PLANES

5 Slide the same flap behind the layer of the Landscape section and start to reform the wing creases of the Landscape.

6 Reform another fold.

7 Reform the right- hand section, tucking the paper within, as on the original design.

8 Reform the main body creases of the Canard, extending the creases through the extra paper of the Landscape.

9 Complete!

FLIGHT ADVICE

Launch, trim, and creative suggestions
By now, I hope you can work these out for yourselves!

How to hold your plane

Index

Credits

Thanks to: Sarah and David King and Colin Bowling.
To Michael LaFosse, Rikki Donachie, Kunihiko Kasahara and Robin Glynn for allowing their designs to be published. Alison, Daisy, Nick, Gomez, Matilda, Big Dave and Bob, all part of my extended family. John, Mick and Joe for helping keep my fingers flexible. To paper-folders everywhere for their fellowship and inspiration and willingness to share ideas; and Ken Blackburn for pushing paper airplane records to the limit and beyond!

The Author: *Nick Robinson*
An IT lecturer, web author and writer, Nick lives in Sheffield, England. He has been folding for over twenty years and is a council member of the British Origami Society. He also maintains their web site and edits their magazine. He has appeared on television in the UK and abroad and has created numerous designs for magazine, television and other media. Over 150 of his original origami creations have been published in 15 countries around the world. His website is www.12testing.net. As a former professional musician he still performs live, solo improvised ambient guitar concerts.

Origami Contacts:
If you enjoy folding the projects in this book, you really should contact your nearest origami society. They can supply you with paper, new designs, a newsletter and most importantly, many new friends!

Origami USA: www.origami-usa.org

British Origami Society: www.britishorigami.org.uk